PREFIX: em

MEANING: to cause

EXAMPLE: embolden

PREFIX: en

MEANING: to cause

EXAMPLE: enjoy

PREFIX: im

MEANING: not, the opposite of

EXAMPLE: impure

PREFIX: in

MEANING: not, the opposite of

EXAMPLE: incorrect

PREFIX: pre

MEANING: before

EXAMPLE: pregame

PREFIX: re

MEANING: again

EXAMPLE: retry

PREFIX: sub

MEANING: under

EXAMPLE: submarine

PREFIX: un

MEANING: not, the opposite of

EXAMPLE: uncool

Me First!
Prefixes Lead the Way

by
Robin Pulver

illustrated by
Lynn Rowe Reed

Holiday House / New York

It was **PRE**dawn. The classroom was **UN**occupied. Or was it?

Mr. Wright promised to REview PREfixes today.

I'm IMpatient!

The small groups of letters known as **PRE**fixes were stirring.

While we're waiting,
let's REview our cheer.

They pulled out their little horns and tooted:

Tum-te-tum-te-tum!

We are the PREfixes and no one could be prouder.
If you cannot hear us, we'll REyell a little louder.
We know we're great because we go first.
We're so proud we're ready to burst.

re

non

com

en

un

sub

Tooty-tooty-toot-toot-toot!

We attach to words and change what they mean.
We're the greatest leaders you've ever seen!
Forget the rest! Begin with the best! Prefixes!

The **PRE**fixes were **PRE**pared.

We'll lead root words
to a new meaning.

But then the
UNexpected happened.

President Abraham Lincoln opened the door and walked into the room.

He sat down at Mr. Wright's desk, **UN**bent his knees and stretched out his long legs.

I'd DISbelieve this if I weren't seeing it with my own eyes!

He wrote something on a piece of paper and dropped it into his stovepipe hat.

I'm UNsure. This is most UNusual. Is it really him?

NONsense! Abraham Lincoln is dead.

Well, he's UNdead now.

Maybe we're REliving history.

The appearance of President Lincoln was UNexplained . . .

"I wanted to be **UN**recognizable!" said Mr. Wright.
He **RE**moved the beard and rubbed his chin.

Now that he has DEbearded himself, I know it's Mr. Wright.

We were MISled.

"Because," said Mr. Wright, "today is Leadership Day in our school. President Lincoln is an example of a great leader from history."

The **PRE**fixes blew their horns and stomped their feet. **UN**fortunately, they were **UN**heard and **UN**noticed.

What does *humble* mean?
When you're humble, you don't brag and blow your own horn.
The best leaders want to use their talents to help others.
Better make our horns DISappear.
dis
em
com

Abe loved to read, so he walked long distances to borrow books.

He was poor, but when a book he borrowed got ruined by rain, he worked hard to pay for it. He was honest and responsible.
We're never DIShonest or IRresponsible!
We would never leave a book out in the rain.
That is UNthinkable.
dis
ir
de
pre
un

Lincoln told good jokes and stories.
Yes, and like all good leaders, he was a good listener, too. He was friendly and caring and helpful. Good leaders set good examples.

The prefixes listened carefully to everything
Mr. Wright said about being good leaders.

President Lincoln's leadership changed history.
Our leadership changes the meanings of words.
re
non

To open a backpack, kids may need me. I turn *zip* into ***UN**zip*.
If a computer has a bug, I come in handy and change *bug* into ***DE**bug*.
un
de
Good leaders work well with others.
ir
en
WE DO TOO!
anti
em
dis
de

The prefixes couldn't believe how long they had to wait for their turn.

It's UNfair!

un

non

pre

in

UNable to wait any longer, they rushed and stumbled over each other to attach to words. They didn't care which word they found.

anti lunch

sub school

dis book

re pencil

This is IMpossible!
They must be joking! I love a good joke.
Whoops, guess we're being OVEReager.
m
en
over
com

Mr. Wright reached for his stovepipe hat. "Lincoln used to say he felt **UN**dressed without this."

When he put the hat on his head, a folded paper fell out.

"Good grief! I forgot!" he exclaimed. "Today we're supposed to **RE**view **PRE**fixes. Thank goodness Lincoln gave me the idea to keep **RE**minders in my stovepipe hat."

- Review prefixes
- Grade papers
- Buy milk

The **PRE**fixes shivered with excitement.

"Remember," said Mr. Wright, "words that look long and hard to read are often short words with attachments like prefixes and suffixes."

But **UN**like suffixes, we *never* change the spellings of our root words.

If we did, we would be **DIS**obeying the rules of grammar.

Mr. Wright told the kids to search the room for **PRE**fixes. "Then write two sentences about what you would do to help or make a difference if you were a leader. Use your **PRE**fixes. Surprise me!"

The **PRE**fixes made themselves easy to find.
They were ready to **UN**leash their power.

I would have the power to help the whole class DISappear. Then we would REappear suddenly and surprise Mr. Wright.

I would lead an expedition in an ANTIfreeze SUBmarine to UNlock the secrets of the North Pole.

I would lead groups of PREschool kids back to PREhistoric times so they could learn about dinosaurs. But I would not let the kids be UNsafe.

I would UNveil a new fashion of stovepipe hats for everyone. Then we could REcycle our backpacks.

I would RE-create the world so that animals would not go extinct. Too many animals are UNappreciated and UNcared for.

We are the PREfixes.
Humble, helpful leaders!
Watch for us
to be great readers!
ir
de
en
Tun tum
te tum!

 and  are the most commonly used prefixes.

uni and **bi** and **tri** are prefixes, too.

As in **UNI**cycle, **BI**cycle and **TRI**cycle.

Also **BI**weekly and **TRI**weekly.

Prefixes are groups of letters that attach to the front of words and change their meanings. If you know **PRE**fixes you can **UN**lock the meanings of many words.

The "pre" in **PRE**fix is a prefix itself. It means "go before." It's in front of the word "fix" because in this case "fix" means "attach." So a prefix is a group of letters that is attached to the front of a word and changes its meaning.

President Lincoln really did keep messages and reminders in his stovepipe hat.

*This is for Amy Jo Metzendorf, yoga instructor, who reminds me
to breathe and, like prefixes, begin again and again and again.*
—R.P.

To Dorian and Sebastian
—L.R.R.

Text copyright © 2016 by Robin Pulver
Illustrations copyright © 2016 by Lynn Rowe Reed
All Rights Reserved
HOLIDAY HOUSE is registered in the U.S. Patent and Trademark Office.
Printed and bound in April 2016 at Toppan Leefung, DongGuan City, China.
The illustrations were created in mixed media.
www.holidayhouse.com
First Edition
1 3 5 7 9 10 8 6 4 2

Library of Congress Cataloging-in-Publication Data
Names: Pulver, Robin, author. | Reed, Lynn Rowe, illustrator.
Title: Me first! : prefixes lead the way / by Robin Pulver ; illustrated by Lynn Rowe Reed.
Description: New York : Holiday House, [2016] | Summary: "A group of prefixes
have trouble patiently waiting for Mr. Wright to teach a lesson about them
in this introduction to prefixes"— Provided by publisher.
Identifiers: LCCN 2015040850 | ISBN 9780823436446 (hardcover)
Subjects: | CYAC: English language—Suffixes and prefixes—Fiction. | Schools—Fiction.
Classification: LCC PZ7.P97325 Me 2016 | DDC [E]—dc23 LC record available at http://lccn.loc.gov/2015040850

PREFIX: anti

MEANING: against

EXAMPLE: antiwar

PREFIX: com

MEANING: together, with

EXAMPLE: compress

PREFIX: de

MEANING: remove, away from

EXAMPLE: debug

PREFIX: dis

MEANING: not, the opposite of

EXAMPLE: disagree

PREFIX: ir

MEANING: not, the opposite of

EXAMPLE: irregular

PREFIX: mis

MEANING: wrong or badly

EXAMPLE: misspell

PREFIX: non

MEANING: not, the opposite of

EXAMPLE: nonfiction

PREFIX: over

MEANING: too much, above, during

EXAMPLE: overeat